GHOSTS UNLIMITED

A groaning coffin of poems, jokes, riddles, and plots
opened up by Andrew Fusek Peters

Illustrated by Nathan Reed

OXFORD
UNIVERSITY PRESS

OXFORD
UNIVERSITY PRESS

Great Clarendon Street, Oxford OX2 6DP

Oxford University Press is a department of the University of Oxford.
It furthers the University's objective of excellence in research, scholarship,
and education by publishing worldwide in

Oxford New York

Auckland   Cape Town   Dar es Salaam   Hong Kong   Karachi
Kuala Lumpur   Madrid   Melbourne   Mexico City   Nairobi
New Delhi   Shanghai   Taipei   Toronto

With offices in

Argentina   Austria   Brazil   Chile   Czech Republic   France   Greece
Guatemala   Hungary   Italy   Japan   Poland   Portugal   Singapore
South Korea   Switzerland   Thailand   Turkey   Ukraine   Vietnam

Oxford is a registered trade mark of Oxford University Press
in the UK and in certain other countries

British Library Cataloguing in Publication Data

Data available

ISBN-13: 978-0-19-276330-3
ISBN-10: 0-19-276330-X

1 3 5 7 9 10 8 6 4 2

Printed in Great Britain by Cox and Wyman Ltd,
Reading, Berkshire

Contents

We All Love Ghosts!   11

SECTION 1 Fred (Who is into Ghosts, Big-time!)   13

What's My Favourite Hobby?   15
Oh, Brother!   17
Top Ten Haunted Spots   18
The Ghost Catalogue   20
How to Tell a Rotten Body   22
A Shape in the Night   23
Dead Funny Jokes   24
The Ghost with No Head   25
The Haunted Biscuit!   26
My Favourite Place   29
The Mansion   30
What I Saw on My First Day at My New School   32
If You Don't Keep in Shape, You'll End Up in This!   33
Barry the Bully   34
What School is Like When You're Different   35
Have You Ever Seen a Ghost?   36
My Grandma   37
A Walk in the Graveyard   38

SECTION 2 Welcome to Ghost School! 41

What's the Point of Ghost School?   44
How to Get into Ghost School   45
How to Be a Ghost in Five Easy Steps—   46
  the Scary Mary Guide
Spooking It   47
The Ghost School Entrance Exam   49
Amazing Mazes Page   50
Ghost School—How Could You Live Without It?   52
Day and Night and Night and Day   53
Ghost School Assembly   55
First Lesson—the Tricks of the Haunting Trade   56
Dead or Alive?   58
What Ghosts Do During Break   59
The Horrible Deaths Bit   60
Mushy Pleas   61
Scary Mary   62
Beastly Brother   62
Ghastly Gran   63
Who Believes in Ghosts These Days?   65
Ghost Complaints   66
What Do Ghosts Eat?   67
Being a Ghost   68
What Am I?   69
Even Poems Get Scared!   70
Where Do Ideas Come From? A Spooky Explanation 71

Afternoon Sports   72
SBD (Silent But Deadly)   74
Test in Peace   76
Homework Was Never Like This at Home!   77
Dinner Time   78
The Day the Inspectres Called—a Tongue-twister   79
A Night in the Life of a Ghost   80
Do Ghosts Go to the Loo?   80
Bedtime in Ghost School   81
Top Five Favourite Ghost Books   82
School Mottoes Through the Ages   83
The Portraits Page   84
Ghost Rules   86
Use Your Loaf   87
A Very 'Armful Poem   87
Framed!   88
The Mouse's Tail   88
The Problem with Ghost School   89
How to Tell a Human from Five Paces   92
Ghost School Matron   93
Mary to the Rescue   95
Fred's Training Session for Ghosts   96
Goodbye to Ghost School   98

SECTION 3 Return to the Real World 101

Excitement Ahead 102
Time Doesn't Fly 103
Home, Sweet Home 104
There's Something Strange Happening . . . 106
Help! Our School is Haunted! 108
Barry (Stupid as Ever) 110
Fred's Revenge 112
You've Got Company! 114
The Ghosts Are Back in Town (a Dead Cool Rap) 116
It's Goodbye from Fred 118

Index of Titles and First Lines 120
Answers 125
About Andrew Fusek Peters 127

We All Love Ghosts!

Welcome to this spooky book,
Dare to take a closer look!
As we all love ghosts!

Who wants to spend an evening bored?
Jump to the creak of an old floorboard,
As we all love ghosts!

What's that sudden slam of a door?
Look at those goosebumps! Give us more!
As we all love ghosts!

Flick these pages, check them out
But don't blame me if you can't get out!
For we all love ghosts!

Beware the haunts of poetry
And don't say 'Bet you can't scare me!' (WE WILL!)
As we all love ghosts!

Fred
(Who is into Ghosts, Big-time!)

What's My Favourite Hobby?

I'm not into skateboards, or computer games
But love those lists of obituary names.

Some children simply like to play,
But I want to know who passed away . . .

A game of footy? A little bike ride?
I'd much rather play Jekyll and Hyde!

My mum and dad think I'm totally mad,
And that I'm possessed by a stupid fad!

My little brother is such a pain,
He's convinced that I'm insane!

And yes, I'll admit that I'm obsessed
With those who have taken eternal rest.

The hero of this journey? That's me—I'm Fred
And I just hope you're not scared of the dead . . .

Every crack of dawn and without fail,
I pick up my copy of the Daily Wail

My favourite is the 'Top Ten Haunted Spots'!
And 'How Long Before A Body Rots'.

This hobby has grabbed me by the throat,
I mean, who wants to walk, when you can float?

I hope you don't mind if I brag or boast,
That I'm an expert when it comes to the ghost!

This is my boring dad. (When he hides behind the paper, I'm not sure if he's alive or dead most of the time. And his snores are so loud they make things move mysteriously!)

My boring mum. (I talk, she never listens. I might as well be a poltergeist.)

Oh, Brother!

He's the burglar, he's the nicker,
and the thief of all my stuff
who drives me up the wall
until I scream, 'I've had enough!'
He's quick to get in trouble,
even quicker not to linger
and guess who gets the blame
when he points his little finger?
So let me stop this poem
as I pause to catch my breath
to think of different ways
for my bro to meet his death!

And my little pain
of a brother—
nickname BOD
(Better Off Dead).
All too alive for
my liking.

Top Ten Haunted Spots

At Home

Under the bed (every single night)
Behind the curtain (is the window shut tight?)
Outside the window (a tree branch creaking?)
On the stairs (a floorboard squeaking?)
Up in the attic (I'm sure I heard a groan)

At School

In the boys' loo, (the door suddenly slamming)
In the girls' loo (the evidence is damning)
At the edge of the playground (just behind that tree)
Turn round quickly (it's behind me!)
Out of the corner of my eye (I know I'm not alone . . .)

19

The Ghost Catalogue

Ghosts at midnight, once a year,
Ghosts who specialize in fear.
Ghosts that pop up once a week,
Naked ghosts who love to streak!

Ghosts that whisper like a dream,
Ghosts that love to howl and scream.
Legless, headless, lost their arms,
Ghosts that set off ghost alarms.

Ref 01

Ref 02

Ref 03

Ref 06

Ref 07

Ref 08

They come in every shape and size
But all together, they surprise.
Their colour? From misty
To bright see-through.
Their mission? To pay
A visit to **YOU!**

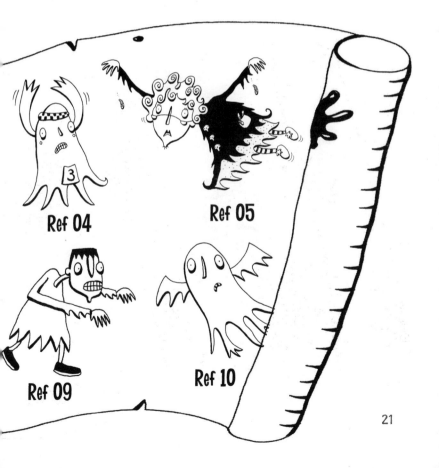

Ref 04

Ref 05

Ref 09

Ref 10

How to Tell a Rotten Body

Somewhat stinky, covered in flies,
Maggots squirming out of the eyes
Shake its hand (you know the rest . . .)
If it comes off, it's passed the test!

A Shape in the Night

I flutter and flit and find my way round

without a whisper or a sound.

I'm a cut-out shadow of night and the truth is that

though I fly fast, I'm blind as a bat.

That's because you are a bat!

I've got a secret book of Dead Funny Jokes under my bed at home. It's spooktacular!

Dead Funny Jokes

What is a ghost's favourite food?
Ghoul-ash

How do ghosts greet each other?
Howl do you do?

Why do ghosts like going to the pub?
They are licensed to serve spirits!

The Ghost with No Head

The ghost who has a chopped-off head,
Likes to moan right under my bed.
But I'm not scared he's come to call,
As his bonce makes the perfect ball.
Watch it dribble across the floor,
What a header! What a score!

Ghosts are great to use as an excuse—like when I've nicked my mum's last biscuit!

The Haunted Biscuit!

'I was haunted by that biscuit,
You have to understand,
How it suddenly crept up on me
And landed in my hand . . . '

My mother wagged her finger
And fixed me with her eyes!
'But it leaped out from the larder.
I'm not telling any lies!

'The only way to stop it
From making crumbs of me,
Was to bite its yummy head off,
Then drown it in my tea!'

My mum agreed politely,
Pretending that she cared:
'It's no more spooky biscuits, love,
For I don't want you scared!'

Haunted by a biscuit?
This isn't what I planned.
Now I'm haunted by the longing
For a biscuit in my hand.

When my family is driving me mad,
I like to get away for a stroll
and think about my favourite subject,
and there's only one place I can do that!

My Favourite Place

I have to admit the nearest beach
Is too many miles out of my reach.
The local park? I'm afraid it's true
It's filled with dogs and their . . . you know (don't you?).
There's only one place I like to be:
Yes! That's right! The cemetery.
I can't hang with my mates down the rec. Instead
I prefer the chilled-out company of the dead.
Admittedly, you don't get much conversation
Sitting on the slab of a dead relation,
But I like the quiet slowness of pace,
Yes, the graveyard is my favourite place.

I love walking past this place on the way to school—
nothing like an empty house to start off my day.
It seems to have been there forever ...

The Mansion

The house stood still like a solitary crane
In a pool of deep green grass.
The windows dark as thundered rain,
Rooms all drowned in glass.

Memories have come to roost,
And shadows gobble the light,
Here, the house is now a ghost,
Visited by the fox of night.

House that once held charm and chime
Now a bricked-up box of air.
The thief has come and stolen time,
The silence dies, there's no one there.

This house a washed-up lonely shell
On the grey and windswept lea.
But cup your ear and listen well
To the hiss of the far-off sea.

School is weird if you're a ghost-lover like me. You look at things in a different way (and let your imagination run wild)!

What I Saw on My First Day at My New School

At the end of school,
All the pupils vanished . . . like ghosts, I guess.
I was all alone when
I heard a shuffling sound in the corridor.
Closer and closer,
It crept up on me,
Slowly, slowly
The stench of its breath,
As it wafted into my nostrils, nearly strangled me to death.
Then I saw it!
Un-be-liev-able!
It dribbled and drooled. It was disgusting!
Two eyes rolled round in their sockets,
A lizard-like tongue slithered out from
Cracked lips,
And, for some reason,
Huge flakes of snow fell from its greasy hair.
I wanted to run, but my feet were buried in the ground.

It was then that the creature said,

'Welcome to our school,
I'm the Head!'

If You Don't Keep in Shape, You'll End Up in This!

No matter if you do your best, or win the prize, or pass the test,

Have you guessed? I'll leave you to fill out the rest!! . . . .

you'll end up here!

33

Oh no, here comes Barry, the school bully.

Barry the Bully

Barry? Yeah, that's me, I'm always
Right, as you can see.
Anyhow, today we got this boy—he
Is bananas and doesn't fool me.
Not quite my normal cup of tea.
Learn to like him? How can that be?
E's in love with ghosts, oh deary me!
Safe to say, he's off his trolley.
Smiles get lost! How dare he be jolly!

Time to make 'is life a misery,
We'll cure 'is strange insanity,
I'll duff up 'is reality.
That'll sort him, just you see!

Barry was spreading lies
about me and laughing
his head off
(I wish).

34

What School is Like When You're Different
(The Ghost-Lover's Lament)

Fingers point like claws,
Lips wriggle into terrifying frowns,
Insults float through the air like spectres,
Their laughter is unreal and unearthly,
As they close round me,
I'm taunted and haunted by their bullying:

'Fred's in love with a spook,
That lives inside the bog!
His ghoulfriend is a spectre,
And he'd like to give her a snog!'

Have You Ever Seen a Ghost?

Oh, just to
Glimpse a Ghoul
Snaffle a sight
Of a tiny Sprite!

Oh, just to
Speak with a Spectre
Or simply boast
Of one little Ghost!

Oh, just to
Spot a Spirit
I'd be made
If I snapped a Shade!

But instead
I really don't know
And the Nothing I find
Might be all in my mind.

My Grandma

My grandma's gone away
And left her empty chair,
I cross my fingers and pray,
But she's no longer there.

We're all as sad as clowns,
We cry and our noses go red,
We live in a land of frowns,
For all of our laughter is dead.

I miss her crinkly face,
Her hands so creased and worn,
There's no one to take her place,
Oh, my heart is tumbled and torn.

I wonder if she hears
As I sit in her comfy chair.
She'd wipe away my tears,
Sing **Hush, my dear, there, there.**
Sing **Hush, my dear, there, there.**

I was in the graveyard one evening. Nothing like hanging out with the dead to perk you up!

A Walk in the Graveyard

As I wandered past each shadowy tomb,
It wasn't the graveyard that filled me with doom.
At least I felt safe in the cemetery
Though Barry's cruel laughter haunted me.
He thinks that spectres don't exist,
But there has to be a clue he's missed . . .
I strolled along through the midnight clear
But missed my footing and fell oh dear !!!

If you want
to find out more,
solve this riddle
to open the door.
My first is in Kindness
but not in Hate.
My second in Friend
and also in Mate.
My third is in Yeti
(who might exist).
Now give the answer
a little twist . . .

SECTION 2

Welcome to Ghost School!

Aha! A key!

It was cold enough even to make an iceberg wail. My teeth were clicking so loud, they could be heard in Timbuktu. Hairs rose on the back of my neck, turning me into a porcupine. Goosebumps on my arms grew so big you could ski down them.

SUDDENLY!

Oh, dear me, it's not good you're this late
For that ever so important date!
Do you want me to e-lab-or-ate?
We must rush, or you'll miss your fate!

You what?

The In-spectres will be in a state
And your results will not be that great!

Excuse me, miss, but what are you on about?

My name is Scary Mary and how do you do?
Let's see if you're any good at this? BOO!!

(Didn't know which was more scary—this sudden BOO,
or the fact that Mary was quite see-through!)

I don't mean to appear a total fool,
But you are the candidate for . . .
   Ghost School?

What? Mmm…(Let me think. Opportunity here,
she thinks I'm someone else!)

Yes. That's me. Fred. Fred the Dead.
I tried my best to look very pale
And gave an imitation wail.

Let's look at you closely. Oh, goodness me!
This boy is alive! Now let me see,
A human being! How can we fool
The cruel examiners of this Ghost School?

What do you mean? I'm dead as a dodo,
I've kicked the bucket! My breath is a no-no.
(I tried to hold my breath…to no longer be
But see-through Mary saw through me!)

What's the Point of Ghost School?

Let's face it, some ghosts are not so terrifying,
In fact, the humans end up crying
(with laughter).

They might have worked for years and years
On the best way to reduce their victims to tears
(of horror).

And so these spirits need a new direction
And a truly terrifying education
(or they will go nowhere).

If they don't want to end up the fool
Then what they need is Ghost School
(our motto—we dare to scare!).

How to Get into Ghost School

You see . . .

If you want to get into Ghost School,
There is one qualification
Which doesn't involve writing answers
Or sitting an examination.

You don't have to practise your BOO!
Or recite your most hair-raising lines.
We simply ask your permission
To check for a few vital signs.

When it comes to studying you closely,
Check your mouth, feel your wrist, prod your eyes,
Just trust us, there's no point pretending
You're scary. We'll see through your lies.

You might have worked hard for months
On a spine-tingling composition
But we only want evidence
Of some serious de-composition.

If you're stuck, here is one helpful hint,
A clue for how you get ahead,
Our school requires one simple rule:
That each of its pupils be

Fred, we have to work on the human angle. Your job in this exam is not to be dead good but good at being dead!

How to Be a Ghost in Five Easy Steps— the Scary Mary Guide

1. The big-white-sheet-on-the-head technique is so last year. Nobody will be fooled. Torn T-shirt with slimy ketchup stains is far better.

2. Practise moaning. Every moan should be a work of art. If the person you are groaning at puts their hands over their ears and doubles over in agony, you know you are getting there.

3. A good bit of dribbling helps. (If you think we are talking football here, you will never reach the Premier Phantom Division.)

4. Stare without blinking for a long time. (This is what dead people are brilliant at. It hurts, but you'll get used to it.)

5. Finally, work hard on your shuffling (not playing cards, you fool!). Arms out in front—think Granny meets Snail and you're in with a chance.

Good luck! Here's a spare rotting thumb to slide on. The transparency issue is more difficult. Just try not to shake anyone's hand and only open doors when no one is looking. As for resembling a rotting vegetable, a bit of stinky make-up should do the trick.

Spooking It

First I had to pretend
to be a ghost.

I had the look just right.

The smell was enough to
make stink bombs jealous.

WHOOAAHH

I moaned beautifully.

I dribbled all over the place.

I stared until my eyeballs nearly popped out.

I shuffled like a well-behaved zombie.

And for convincers, I showed them my add-on rotting thumb.

Then there was the written test. That was fun!

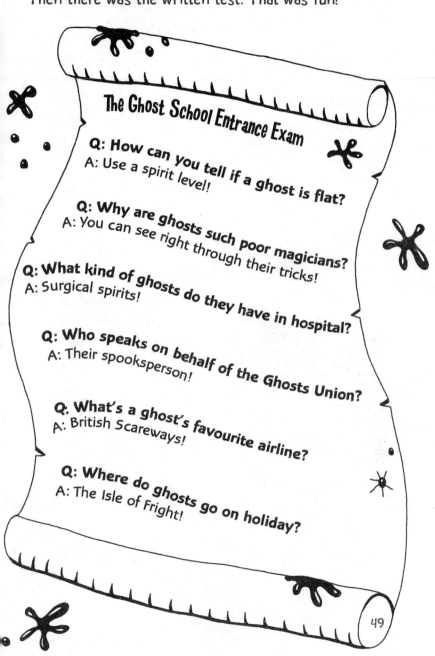

The Ghost School Entrance Exam

Q: How can you tell if a ghost is flat?
A: Use a spirit level!

Q: Why are ghosts such poor magicians?
A: You can see right through their tricks!

Q: What kind of ghosts do they have in hospital?
A: Surgical spirits!

Q: Who speaks on behalf of the Ghosts Union?
A: Their spooksperson!

Q. What's a ghost's favourite airline?
A: British Scareways!

Q: Where do ghosts go on holiday?
A: The Isle of Fright!

I've passed! I'm through (but not see-through).
Soon, I'll get my Degree in **Boo!**

Amazing Mazes Page

And every ghost, like a snail,
Leaves an ectoplasmic trail.
Simply use your finger to trace
Your way through this slimy place.
Just one leads to the Ghost School gate,
Find it or meet a gruesome fate!

Ghost School—How Could You Live Without It?

WELCOME TO GRAVEYARD HIGH!
IT'S THE SCHOOL THAT REALLY IS COOL!

Set on its own, on top of a hill,
Surrounded by acres of skeletal trees,
Ghost School has views
Which are guaranteed to take your death away.
It is built with the latest technology:
Floorboards have built-in creakability,
Hinges screech no matter how much you oil them,
And every room has air-conditioning (no windows).
There is an unpleasant selection of attics and basements.
Cobwebs are provided free of charge.
After a hard night of haunting,
Pupils can take a dip in the swimming ghoul,
They can send an e-wail or two
And then slip into their sunken beds
(No coffin allowed)
and
Rest In Peace.

Day and Night and Night and Day

Wow, this place is ever so strange,
as day and night have had an exchange.
They get up at night, to start their day,
then sleep the whole of the day away

Ghost School Assembly

Welcome to Fred
Who's recently dead,
His accident,
Just wasn't meant,
His spirit feels tender
From a fight with a blender!
So, spectres, please
Do make him at ease,
As our little school
Is really dead cool!

55

First Lesson—the Tricks of the Haunting Trade

Good evening, pupils,
Tonight we shall try
To learn new ways
To terrify!

Now split into pairs.
Jim! No, not you!
Did you hear me say
'Cut yourself in two'?

I don't care if you dream
Of impressing Heather,
Jim! It's not funny!
Pull yourself together!

Scaring takes skill—
Whispering in ears,
Creeping up in toilets,
Conjuring fears!

Mary, oh, really!
My impatience grows,
There's nothing scary
Inside your nose!

Bogeymen will always
Hit the horror spot,
But a bogey's a bogey,
And haunting it's **not**!

Now listen up, all,
I want without fail
To hear every one of you
Practise your wail.

Luckily, I got to work with Mary! Even if she did like a bit of nose-picking! Phew! She gave me loads of tips. And soon I was ready to scare with the best of them.

Dead or Alive?

It's one thing to be a Scarer
But another to be the Scaree
If I had a choice in the matter
I know which one I'd be!

What Ghosts Do During Break

You guessed it, the riddle's not hard,
Break is taken in the (grave)yard.
Leap-frogging? There's plenty of stones
And the climbing frame is made of bones.
I spy? Beginning with T? Tomb!
Try some exploring in the catacomb.
The eco-garden has been newly laid
And planted out with deadly nightshade.
I'm out of breath (not completely!) with all that play,
Beginning to think I might even stay!

At break, I was introduced to some of my fellow pupils.

The Horrible Deaths Bit

You wouldn't think this was a school.
I mean, this place is really cool!
(Freezing in fact!) Lessons in haunting
Are much more fun than bully-taunting.
It's a bit odd to get your head
Round the fact that everyone's dead.
Met a bunch of great new mates,
Who told me how they met their fates.
I found it difficult not to laugh
When each one read me their epitaph!

Mushy Pleas

Doris Perkins loved to chat
As she stirred that mushy vat;
But she gave a muffled shout
That day her dentures slithered out.
This is why she came to grief
Trying to retrieve her teeth.
She fell in with a little plop
And her days came to a stop.
So put your hands together, please,
And pray for Doris, Rest In Peas.

Scary Mary

Wonder why her nose
is squashed?
And her face a bit
bish-boshed?
She fell from a cliff.
Owwwww . . . Splat!
For Mary that was the
end of that.

Beastly Brother

Little bro
drove me insane,
picked his nose
to be a pain.
Let us pray
for brother Wayne,
sneezed so hard,
blew out his brain.

ACHOO!

62

Ghastly Gran

Ghastly Gran,
ever so mean,
ended up in
the washing machine.
Don't mean
to make you wince,
but she always dreamed
of a purple rinse.
No longer am I terrified,
for ghostly Gran
has spun and died.

Who Believes in Ghosts These Days?

We've got gismos, gadgets, mobile phones,
What do we want with a bunch of bones?
No, we don't believe in ghosts!

There's Hi-Fi, Wi-Fi, MP3,
TV, DVD, Recordable CD,
So forget your belief in ghosts!

With the latest, greatest techno-stuff
There's no point vanishing in a huff,
As we don't believe in ghosts!

Stick a city map on a memory card
Build an office on the old graveyard
Yeah, we don't believe in ghosts!

Listen up, right, this world's too busy,
No point spirits getting in a tizzy,
For we don't believe in ghosts!

Science provides exp-la-nation
And the rest? Ima-gin-ation,
Cos we don't believe in ghosts!

Ghost School seems
an unhappy place.
Maybe Freddy can
solve this case!

Ghost Complaints

We aim to cause
Disaster and distress,
But get third prize
For our fancy dress!

We try out our best
Spine-chilling moans:
They think it's a cat
And throw down stones.

We howl and growl,
But to our indignation
Everyone blames their
Imagination!

Nobody believes us!
Save the Wail!
In the test of fear,
We've been given a fail.

Me too.

I began to feel sorry for my phantasmic friends
I mean, they've already had such horrible ends!
But to have a human like Barry laugh in your face?
There must be a way to deal with this disgrace!
You see, I'm beginning to like this bunch
But first, it's time for a spot of lunch.

What Do Ghosts Eat?

For starters:
Cold-sweat soup (nicely chilled)

For main course:
Roast stake with grave-y

For pudding:
Apple tremble with i-scream

To drink:
A nice strong cup
of coffin

Also available:
Dread and butter
Hand sandwiches

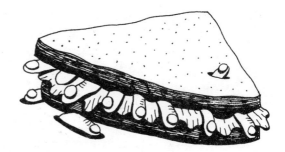

Later I got chatting to Old Gran (you know, the one who fought with a washing machine, and lost). She's a wise old bird. And always smells so clean, unlike me.

Being a Ghost

Let me tell you, Fred,
Afterlife is like the pudding
At the end of a fantastic meal.
I mean, who needs bodies, eh?
They ache and keep going wrong.
No matter how many times you service them
They always break down in the end.
Not only that, but having a body means you have
To go to work, pay the bills,
Feed the washing machine/kids/parking meter.
No, being a ghost is the life for me.
Walls in the way? No probs.
Fancy a bit of solo flying? Easy peasy.
Revenge on the bullies? Just wait till they see you
In the middle of the night!
I miss the food, I suppose. Can't beat a nice cuppa tea.
And cuddles, nice warm soft ones. Hmmm.
Still a ghost's gotta do what a ghost's gotta do.
Ta-ra then.

What Am I?

My heart's a-flutter, my spirit's torn
When I think of the tree where I was born.
The sad, four-cornered truth is that
Even now I feel so flat.
I am in shreds, so incomplete,
In death I've stayed as white as a sheet.
Was I buried? No, it was a sin
That I was crumpled and chucked in the bin.
Can you guess why I'm covered in creases?
Pray for me, I'm Ripped in Pieces!

Answer on page 125!

Being in Ghost School does make you think. What if everything has a ghost—a bit like a shadow?

Even Poems Get Scared!

Help!
I'm only a little poem,
All alone on this huge page.
Listen? Can you hear that sound,
Out beyond all that white space?
Oh! It's only an exclamation mark!
I'm scared and so I run through a long, winding
     sentence,
Full of sharp, horrible clauses
That go on
And on
And on
Forever,
Until at last,
I come to a friendly full stop.

I'm trapped inside this book!
Can you hear me?

CAN YOU HEAR ME?

Maybe I'm a figment or a fragment? A ghost-poem?
Written long ago by a writer,
I'm dead as dust
And now only haunting your mind . . .

(But my ideas are as alive and fresh
As wriggling worms—so watch out!)

Where Do Ideas Come From? A Spooky Explanation

Good ideas are like ghosts,
They creep up on you when you least expect it.
You could be in the bath,
Walking along the street,
Being told off by a teacher,
Picking the wax from your ears,
When:

BAM!

The idea has knocked you sideways,
Blown you away,
Sent shivers (by first-class mail) down your spine
And then you are possessed,
Haunted by inspiration.
You forget to eat,
Turn white as a sheet,
Spend time moaning and groaning.

The only cure is to
Grab a pen
And stab the poor, innocent white sheets of flowing paper
Until they bleed with lyrical ink.
At last,
Like Frankenstein,
You have brought dead words to life
And they can go and leap out from
The fluttering wings of a book
And haunt somebody else,
For good ideas are like ghosts . . .

After all that thinking, I was ready to go down to the sports pitch for afternoon games.

Afternoon Sports

It's Manspectre United versus Chelsee-through!

Wow, what a perfect ghoul!

73

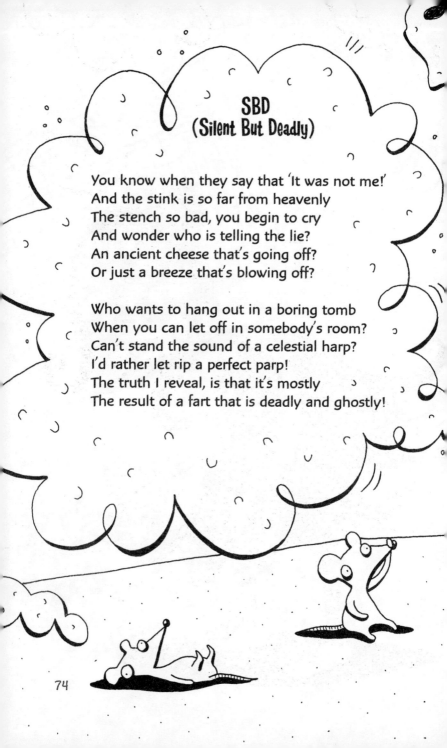

SBD
(Silent But Deadly)

You know when they say that 'It was not me!'
And the stink is so far from heavenly
The stench so bad, you begin to cry
And wonder who is telling the lie?
An ancient cheese that's going off?
Or just a breeze that's blowing off?

Who wants to hang out in a boring tomb
When you can let off in somebody's room?
Can't stand the sound of a celestial harp?
I'd rather let rip a perfect parp!
The truth I reveal, is that it's mostly
The result of a fart that is deadly and ghostly!

Then it was time for homework.

Test in Peace

Ghosts are awful writers!
But it's not as if they care.
Have you tried holding a pencil
When you're made of nothing but air?

Homework Was Never Like This at Home!

Too much prep? The answer is this:
Whisper, whimper, silent hiss.

Doodle, dawdle, endless daydream?
Start with a cry but end with a scream.

Words don't hurt, nor sticks and stones
So master the art of making moans.

By the end of the evening we must deliver
At least one decent, spine-chilling shiver.

Stop that racket!

But, sir, we're doing our groanwork!

At dinner time, there was a lot of joking around.

Dinner Time

What's a must-have gadget for ghosts?
A mobile moan!

What do ghosts like to eat?
Spooogetti!

What room can't a ghost go into?
The living room!

Why did the ghost go to the funfair?
He wanted to go on the rollerghoster!

The Day the Inspectres Called—a Tongue-twister

Even spectres need inspectors,
We expected a spectre inspector,
And the spectre inspector inspected us,
The spectre inspector wore spectacles.
So the spectre inspector in spectacles inspected us.
We had to show the spectre inspector respect.
We expected then respected the inspection
Of the spectre inspector in spectacles.

(Try saying that really, really fast!)

A Night in the Life of a Ghost
(Spot the mistakes!)

Got up,
Had beans-on-ghost
While I read the ghost, delivered by the ghostman.
Went to the library to get out the latest spook.
Ghost chicken for lunch. Dead tasty.
Drove to the ghost (near Shiverpool)
And had a dip in the see (through).
Practised bogey-boarding on some big graves.
Dad was ghost impressed,
Though I don't like to ghost!

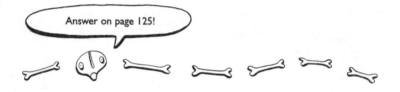

Answer on page 125!

Do Ghosts Go to the Loo?

Though we are invisible,
We still have to go to the loo,
Bit of a pain, more of a strain,
And then, an enormous **BOO!**

Remember, earlier, what I said?
Night takes the place of day instead…

Bedtime in Ghost School

Phew, that was a night!
I'm ready for a good day's rest!
Nice cold bath filled with ectoplasm,
Brush sweetpaste onto teeth (great for long-term rotting),
Clean out maggots in ears,
Drift to nice damp bed in basement while being
   told to hurry up.
Tell terrifying tales about . . . HUMAN BEINGS!
(Don't believe a single word.)
Teacher tells us to keep quiet by wagging his finger at us
(Then he puts it back on).
Lights on. Drift off,
Hoping for some good fright-mares.

zZZZZZZ

In the middle of the day when everyone was asleep, I decided to explore the school. First stop: the library!

Top Five Favourite Ghost Books

Harry Rotter and the Chamber of Spirits
Malice in Underland
Lord of the Things
A Midsummer Night's Scream
Goodnight, Mr Tomb

School Mottoes Through the Ages

It's Cool to be Cool

We Dare to Scare

The Dead! Coming to a neighbourhood near you soon!

The Best at Eternal Rest

Excellence Through Total Terror

The Portraits Page
(Heads Through the Ages)

Harry the Horrible

Harry the Horrible
(Junior)

Harry the Half-Eaten
Horrible (son of Harry
the Horrible and Lady
Fall-in-the-Lake)

Master Eurghhhh

Henry Half-Head the First
(ruled six months)

Derek Decomposing,
son of Derek Drowned

Violet Vaguely
See-Through

Godfrey
the Somewhat Ghoulish

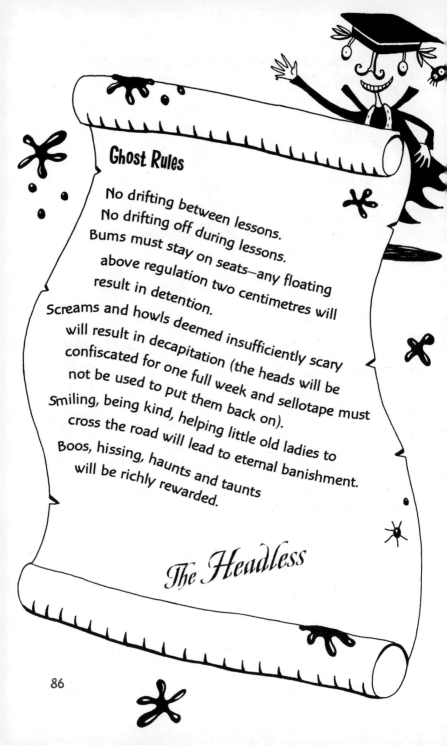

Ghost Rules

No drifting between lessons.

No drifting off during lessons.

Bums must stay on seats—any floating above regulation two centimetres will result in detention.

Screams and howls deemed insufficiently scary will result in decapitation (the heads will be confiscated for one full week and sellotape must not be used to put them back on).

Smiling, being kind, helping little old ladies to cross the road will lead to eternal banishment.

Boos, hissing, haunts and taunts will be richly rewarded.

The Headless

There were all sorts of other strange ghosts lurking about in Ghost School!

Use Your Loaf

Brown or white
I rise in the night
With crumbling toes
And a melted nose
Thick or thin
I lurk in the bin
I am the ghost
Of a piece of toast!

A Very 'Armful Poem

In the old abandoned farm,
Beware the Ghost of the Bleeding Arm,
Hope your feet can carry you faster,
Else she might ask you for a plaster!

Framed!

Let's play the riddle game
And put you in the **frame**
This is my second clue,
I really am **see-through**.
Do you get the joke?
These days I'm **shattered** and **broke**!

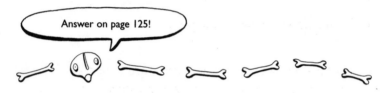

Answer on page 125!

The Mouse's Tail

Saw the cheese, in the trap.
Guess the end. Snip. Snap. Snap.
This is the reason you can see
That now there are the two of me.

Finding my way round Ghost School was hard,
Oh, give me back my old graveyard!

The Problem with Ghost School

As the floorboards sing their symphonic sound
The rooms, like ghosts, follow you around,
So when you've just walked out of one
You're back where you started. It's no fun!
But worst is trying to find just one door—
When you're a ghost, what are they for?
I'm not unhinged, let me give you a clue:
Walls are made for drifting through.
But I'm too solid—I keep bumping my head,
Life would be easier if I was dead.
So what if this place is a murky maze?
It's filled with hidden passageways,
And though I appear to be unprepared,
There are sliding panels for the gliding-impaired.
Mary's lent me the Ghost School Guide,
It's great to have a friend on your side . . .

BOP!

BATTER!

BONG!

It was enough to wake the Dead,
and there they all stood
in front of Fred...

The Headless rolled each of his eyes.

How To Tell a Human from Five Paces

Is this blood that I see
Just a little too runny?

Does it mean you're alive?
Well, I don't find it funny!

You have woken us up
With an un-ghostly scream.

You stink like you're fresh
Yes, you're not what you seem!

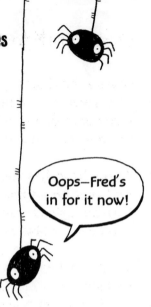

Oops—Fred's in for it now!

Let's face it, you've broken
The unwritten law,

That only the dead
Are allowed through the door.

I've had it with folk
That deny we exist

And this little boy
Well, he'll never be missed!

What's worse, he's a traitor
And I've had enough . . .

So summon the matron
It's time to get tough!

Ghost School Matron

Beware the Ghost School matron,
And never ever smile,
If she doesn't hear you moaning,
You'd better run a mile.

If your heart has started beating
And your symptoms include breath,
This contagious case of perkiness
Can be solved by a dose of death!

She'll strangle you with bandages
And stifle all your screams,
She'll poison you with pills
And snip off all your dreams.

Beware the Ghost School matron
On the days you don't feel ill,
For a healthy ghost stays dead
And she'll make sure you will!

My heart quivered like an arrow.
This was it. End of Fred.
At that moment, I even began to miss my pain
of a brother. I would never see my parents again.
A single tear drifted down my cheek
and leapt like a phantom from my chin
to vanish into the ground.

Mary to the Rescue

Mary, Mary, quite contrary
This is what she said,
I have a very cunning plan!
But Fred must keep his head!

He is the only human
Who believes that we are there
So to make him one of us
Would really be unfair.

This boy can solve our problems
And it turns out he's quite nice,
So I suggest you bend his ear
And ask for Fred's advice!

Matron was disappointed for sure,
As now she couldn't give me
her cure.

Phew! That was a narrow escape!

95

Fred's Training Session for Ghosts
(With Some Help from Mary)

Come on, chant it after me,
Shout it loud, yes, what are we?
With a G-H-O-S-T
The best at UN-REE-AL-I-TEE

Pull that face, work that SCOWL
Fill your lungs for a gruesome HOWL!

Come on, chant it after me,
Shout it loud, yes, one-two-three
With a G-H-O-S-T
The best at UN-REE-AL-I-TEE

Whispers banned, let's hear you shout,
Eyeballs one and two, pop out!

Come on, do your A-B-C,
Shout it loud, yes, what are we?
With a G-H-O-S-T
The best at UN-REE-AL-I-TEE

We are the best at being dead
Make them shiver, swivel that head!

Come on, do your A-B-C,
Shout it loud, yes, what are we?
With a G-H-O-S-T
The best at UN-REE-AL-I-TEE

Right, I think that's enough from Freddy,
Let's just hope these ghosts are ready!
It's time to say my job is done,
I'm ready to go back and have some fun.

Goodbye to Ghost School

All the ghosts were waving goodbye
With a howl and scream and sigh (as usual).
Tears streamed like ectoplasm down my face:
Though I was alive, I'd miss this dead-cool place.
I shook a few transparent hands,
Was I ready to return to the living lands?
Just then, Mary floated up to me:
'Problems at school, or with your family?
Give us a call on your mobile moan,
As you've got ghosts and you're never alone!'
Then, I felt my knees go weak,
As she planted a smacker on my cheek.
Though they might have come to terrible ends,
I'll get by with a little help from my friends!

SECTION 3

Return to the Real World

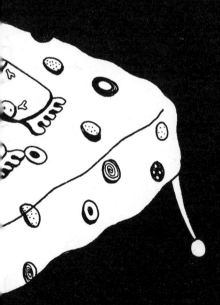

Excitement Ahead
(A Riddle)

My first's in **hello**
but not **goodbye**

My second's in **hi!**
but never in **shy**

My third's in **Fred**
but not in **dead**

My fourth's in **excitement**
and also **ahead**

Answer on page 125!

Time Doesn't Fly

It seems that, in Ghost School,
Time doesn't fly,
I've only been gone
For a blink of an eye!

Home, Sweet Home

Life is great, let me explain . . .
My bro, who thinks I am insane,
Has seen a ghost beneath my bed
And now the brat is filled with dread!
Ghosts are useful, as you see
And now my brother's nice to me!

As for boring household chores,
Well, in my contract, there's a clause
That if I teach the ghosts to scare
They'll do my tidying everywhere.
My parents can't believe their eyes
To see their son so organized.
It's great to see the phantoms roam
All around my Home, Sweet Home!

I was back at school and still they were laughing at me.
Nothing had changed—surprisingly.
Time for Fred to take charge of this case
and (with a little ghostly help)
cause some chaos all over the place!

And next day in school, things started going a
bit strange.

There's Something Strange Happening . . .

Look out of the window when teacher is droning
At the spot just beyond the reach of your eye,
There in the street, where there shouldn't be shadows
Shivering dark beneath the grey sky.

Then hear the breeze blow at the back of the playground
As it hisses the leaves just behind that tree;
Was it wind that slammed the school toilet door
When no one was there at half-past three?

And what of the echoing clatter of footsteps
Through a twilight that suddenly stole the day?
How loud is the heart that beats in your chest
As you run from the fear that follows like a stray?

The moaning and groaning of too many floorboards
That comes from the empty apartment below,
That curtain is flapping, oh, why is it slapping
When the window is closed and there's no wind? Oh no!

You might think you're safe and snug in your bed
But the lights from the street move slowly like glue
As they crawl like insects across the wall,
And get closer

AND

CLOSER

AND

CLOSER

TO

YOU!

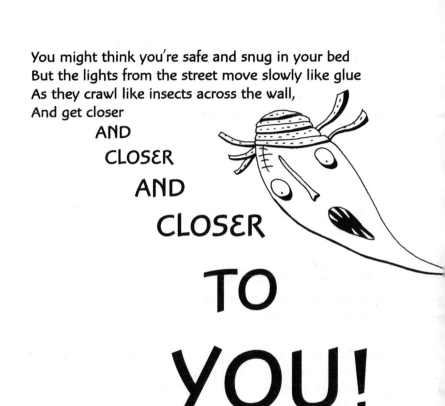

And that was just for starters! The next day, things went even stranger!

Help! Our School is Haunted!

At assembly the Head's hair rose above his head like a helicopter and flew out of the window (it turned out he had a wig). You could say he was tearing his hair out!

Computers skedaddled, leaving empty lonely sockets.

Cups of tea threw themselves to the floor in the staffroom before even tired teachers had a chance to be clumsy.

Shelves full of books that lived in the library moved house overnight to the toilet walls and offered themselves as loo paper.

There were whispers about levitation—especially after Megan Watkins floated past the whole of Year Three one afternoon screaming for her mummy.

To cap it all, the Portakabin vanished overnight. Gone. Not a trace. Not a winkle. Nada. Police had puzzled faces. But all our homework would haunt us no more!

(Hurrah!)

The Head kept saying there must be a rational explanation. He consulted all sorts of brainy boffins, but they came up only with huge question marks.

It couldn't be a severe infestation of ghosts, could it?

Unthinkable!

Barry the Bully was looking very pleased with himself as always. He had flash new trainers and a gold chain round his neck and a flash new mobile phone ringtone:

BLING! BLING!

Barry (Stupid as Ever)

In the playground, he grabbed me by my shirt,
'OK, troll-features, hit the dirt!
I've been having a word with my crew
And we're askin'—is this anything to do with you?'
It was fun to play the innocent lad!
'Don't know what you mean! You must be mad!'
Poor old Barry, how do you explain
The truth to a boy that was born with no brain?
'Well, you'd better stop all these games and stuff,
Or things round here might get a bit rough!'
I stammered, 'Y-y-yes, Barry, you're so right!'
It was time to pay him a visit that night! . . .

Fred's Revenge

I really do not mean to boast,
But it's great hanging out with a friendly ghost.
No need to worry about locks on the door,
Being made of air is a perfect cure!
So there we were, at the end of his bed,
Thinking of ways to fill Barry with dread.
He snuffled, he dribbled, how he snored,
'WAKEY WAKEY!' my friend roared.

I've never seen him so terrified.
'I want my mummy,' the bully cried.
We gave him his wish, it was ever so funny
To see him react to a real mummy.
Barry shook to the roots of his soul
At the mummy wrapped round in toilet roll!
So much for Barry the Bully: he's toast!
It's great hanging out with a friendly ghost!

In fact my new ghost friends turned out to be very useful in all sorts of ways.

You've Got Company!

Parents a problem? Homework not done?
Hire a phantom and have some fun!
A plague of bullies infesting your school?
Or a teacher in love with being cruel?
We promise to send out on a mission
A scheming, screaming apparition!
Our experts in producing fears
Will reduce your enemies to tears!
And once you've paid our modest fee,
You'll get a twelve-month guarantee.
Contact us now, and have some faith
In our new company: Rent-a-Wraith!

Rent-a-Wraith
12-month Guarantee

To: ....

Address: ....
....
....
....

Seriously scary fee: ....

We agree to scheme, scream, put people in tears and fill them with fears!

NOTE TO CUSTOMER:
In the event that our service fails to be satisfactory, we will send you a complimentary sachet of scariness!

115

The Ghosts Are Back in Town (a Dead Cool Rap)

Now put your hands up in the air,
And wave 'em like they're just not there.
It's a party with peril, and a dance of dread,
We are the spectres of street-cred.
Me and my homies, the cold-sweat crew
Cruisin' downtown, just to visit you.

Make ya quiver, quail, quaver, and quake,
You'll be a-shakin' like a heavy earthquake.
No point cryin' or goin' boo-hoo,
We're the ghosts with the mostest and we'll be hauntin' you.
Me and my gang, we own the night,
Tyrants of terror, we're the pharaohs of fright.
Trust me, baby, don't come too near,
Our superpowers will fill ya with fear.
Got a Ph.D. in hauntin', we're qualified
To take the test to the terrified.
We're the petrifying posse, the curdle-milk crew
Wearing out the latest fashion (it's so see-through!)
You'd better run when you see us, dude,
Cos we are the ghouls with attitude!

It's Goodbye from Fred

Dear Reader, time has gone so fast
That this book has breathed its last,
Buried dead inside your head.
But when it's time to go to bed
And you think you're quite alone,
Then listen for a friendly moan.
My poems may not just be lies . . .
You could be in for a surprise!

Night night.

Sleep tight.

Mind the phantoms don't bite!

(First lines are in **bold**)

A Night in the Life of a Ghost	80
A Shape in the Night	23
A Very 'Armful Poem	87
A Walk in the Graveyard	38
Afternoon Sports	72
All the ghosts were waving goodbye	98
Amazing Mazes Page	50
And every ghost, like a snail	50
As I wandered past each shadowy tomb	38
As the floorboards sing their symphonic sound	89
At the end of school	32
Barry (Stupid As Ever)	110
Barry the Bully	34
Barry? Yeah, that's me, I'm always	34
Beastly Brother	62
Bedtime in Ghost School	81
Being a Ghost	68
Beware the Ghost School matron	93
Brown or white	87
Come on, chant it after me	96
Day and Night and Night and Day	53
Dead Funny Jokes	24
Dead or Alive?	58
Dear Reader, time has gone so fast	118
Dinner Time	78
Do Ghosts Go to the Loo?	80

Doris Perkins loved to chat 61

Even Poems Get Scared 70

Even spectres need inspectors 79

Excitement Ahead (A Riddle) 102

Fingers point like claws 35

First Lesson—the Tricks of the Haunting Trade 56

Framed! 88

Fred's Revenge 112

Fred's Training Session for Ghosts 96

Ghastly Gran 63

Ghastly Gran, ever so mean 63

Ghost Complaints 66

Ghost Rules 86

Ghost School Assembly 55

Ghost School—How Could You Live Without It? 52

Ghost School Matron 93

Ghosts are awful writers! 76

Ghosts at midnight, once a year 20

Good evening, pupils 56

Good ideas are like ghosts 71

Goodbye to Ghost School 98

Got up, / Had beans-on-ghost 80

Have You Ever Seen a Ghost? 36

Help! 70

Help! Our School is Haunted! 108

He's the burglar, he's the nicker 17

Home, Sweet Home 104

Homework Was Never Like This at Home! 77

How to Be a Ghost in Five Easy Steps—

the Scary Mary Guide 46

How to Get into Ghost School 45

How to Tell a Human from Five Paces 92

How to Tell a Rotten Body 22

I flutter and flit and find my way round 23

I have to admit the nearest beach 29

I really do not mean to boast 112

I was haunted by that biscuit 26

If You Don't Keep in Shape, You'll End Up in This! 33

If you want to find out more 39

I'm not into skateboards, or computer games 15

In the old abandoned farm 87

In the playground, he grabbed me by my shirt 110

Is this blood that I see 92

It seems that in Ghost School 103

It's Goodbye from Fred 118

It's one thing to be a Scarer 58

Lack-of-breath Day to you! 59

Let me tell you, Fred 68

Let's face it, some ghosts are not so terrifying 44

Let's play the riddle game 88

Life is great, let me explain . . . 104

Little bro drove me insane 62

Look out of the window when teacher
   is droning 106

Mary, Mary, quite contrary 95

Mary to the Rescue 95

Mushy Pleas 61

My Favourite Place 29

My first's in hello 102

My Grandma 37

My grandma's gone away 37

My heart's a-flutter, my spirit's torn 69

No drifting between lessons 86

No matter if you do your best 33

Now put your hands up in the air 116
Oh, Brother! 17
Oh, just to / Glimpse a Ghoul 36
Parents a problem? Homework not done? 114
Phew, that was a night! 81
Saw the cheese, in the trap 88
SBD (Silent But Deadly) 74
Scary Mary 62
School Mottoes Through the Ages 83
Set on its own, on top of a hill 52
Somewhat stinky, covered in flies 22
Spooking It 47
Test in Peace 76
The Day the Inspectres Called—a Tongue-twister 79
The Ghost Catalogue 20
The Ghost School Entrance Exam 49
The ghost who has a chopped-off head 25
The Ghost With No Head 25
The Ghosts Are Back in Town (a Dead Cool Rap) 116
The Haunted Biscuit! 26
The Horrible Deaths Bit 60
The house stood still like a solitary crane 30
The Mansion 30
The Mouse's Tail 88
The Portraits Page 84
The Problem with Ghost School 89
There's Something Strange Happening . . . 106
Though we are invisible 80
Time Doesn't Fly 103
Too much prep? The answer is this 77
Top Five Favourite Ghost Books 82
Top Ten Haunted Spots 18

Under the bed (every single night) 18
Use Your Loaf 87
We aim to cause 66
We All Love Ghosts! 11
Welcome to Fred 55
Welcome to this spooky book 11
We've got gismos, gadgets, mobile phones 65
What Am I? 69
What Do Ghosts Eat? 67
What Ghosts Do During Break 59
What I Saw on My First Day at My New School 32
What School is Like When You're Different 35
What's My Favourite Hobby? 15
What's the Point of Ghost School? 44
Where Do Ideas Come From? A Spooky Explanation 71
Who Believes in Ghosts These Days? 65
Wonder why her nose is squashed? 62
Wow, this place is ever so strange 53
You guessed it, the riddle's not hard 59
You know when they say that 'It was not me!' 74
You see . . . / If you want to get into
 Ghost School 45
You wouldn't think this was a school 60
You've Got Company! 114

Answers

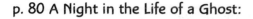

p. 69 What Am I?: a piece of paper

p. 80 A Night in the Life of a Ghost:

Got up,
Had beans-on-**toast**
While I read the **post**, delivered by the **postman**.
Went to the library to get out the latest **book**.
Roast chicken for lunch. Dead tasty.
Drove to the **coast** (near **Liverpool**)
And had a dip in the **sea** (through).
Practised **body-boarding** on some big **waves**.
Dad was **most** impressed,
Though I don't like to **boast**!

p. 88 Framed!: the ghost of a window

p. 102 Excitement Ahead: life

About Andrew Fusek Peters

Andrew Fusek Peters is a poet, author, storyteller, broadcaster, and didgeridoo player, and has written and edited more than forty-five children's titles, including **Ghosts Unlimited** and **Spies Unlimited** for Oxford University Press.

His acclaimed poetry collection **Poems With Attitude** and his verse novel **Crash!** (both with Polly Peters) were longlisted for the Carnegie Medal. His poems have appeared on **Poetry Please, Blue Peter** and the BBC1 poetry series **Wham Bam, Strawberry Jam**, and have been recorded online and on CD for the Poetry Archive, set up by the poet laureate—for more information, visit www.poetryarchive.org.

Andrew lives with his wife Polly and their two children in a converted old chapel in Shropshire.

More details are available on Andrew's books by visiting www.tallpoet.com.

Meet George, super spy.
He has gadgets galore and loves following a
trail—especially if there's a dangerous crook
on the loose!

Crack the codes, and snoop your way around
these fizzing poems, jokes, riddles and plots
from dynamic poet, writer, and broadcaster
Andrew Fusek Peters.

ISBN-13: 978-0-19-276331-0
ISBN-10: 0-19-276331-8